ALPHA BOOKS

POLLUTION

Barbes
Nicola

Pollution

Evans

EVANS BROTHERS LIMITED

This book is based on **Repairing the Damage** *Pollution* by
Alan Collinson, first published by Evans Brothers Limited in
1991, but the original text has been simplified.

Evans Brothers Limited
2A Portman Mansions
Chiltern Street
London W1M 1LE

First published 1995

Typeset by Fleetlines Typesetters, Southend-on-Sea
Printed in Spain by GRAFO, S.A.-Bilbao

ISBN 0 237 51513 X

Acknowledgements

Editor: Rachel Cooke
Language Advisor: Suzanne Tibertius
Design: Neil Sayer
Production: Jenny Mulvanny
Maps: Jillian Luff of Bitmap Graphics
Illustrations: Richard Wise
For permission to reproduce copyright material the author
and publishers gratefully acknowledge the following:
Cover (main picture) Michael Martin, Science Photo Library,
(insets, numbered from top to bottom) 1 Mark Edwards, Still
Pictures, 2, 5 & 6 Allan Collinson, 3 Will McIntyre, Science
Photo Library, 4 Fred Mayer, Magnum
Title page (Mexico City) Mark Edwards, Still Pictures
p4 Joyce Photographics, Planet Earth Pictures p5 (top) David
Reed, Panos Pictures, (bottom) Sebastiao Salgado, Jr,
Magnum p8 Mary Evans Picture Library p9 (top) Ardea
London Ltd p10 Tony Craddock, Science Photo Library p11
Ardea London Ltd, (inset) Lawrence Migdale, Science Photo
Library p12 Fred Mayer, Magnum p13 (top) The Hulton-
Deutsch Collection, (bottom) Burt Glinn, Magnum p16 (top)
Will McIntyre, Science Photo Library, (bottom) Pierre
Schwartz, Sipa-Press/Rex Features p17 Adam Hart Davies,
Science Photo Library p18 Joel Bennett, Survival Anglia p19
(top) Greenwood/ECOSCENE, (bottom) Rapho, Berretty,
Science Photo Library p20 Alan Collinson p21 (top) Mark
Edwards, Still Pictures, (others) Alan Collinson p23 Novosti/
Science Photo Library p24 Novosti/Science Photo Library p26
Rasmussen, Sipa-Press/Rex Features p28 US Dept of Energy/
Science Photo Library p29 (left) e.t. archive, (right) US Dept
of Energy, Science Photo Library p30 Philipe Plailly, Science
Photo Library p31 Alan Collinson p32 (top) Adam Hart-
Davis, Science Photo Library, (bottom) Anthony and
Elizabeth Bomford, Ardea London Ltd p33 Ron Giling,
Panos Pictures p34 Robert Harding Picture Library p35
Michael Martin, Science Photo Library p36 Peter Menzel,
Science Photo Library p37 David Scharf, Science Photo
Library p38 Warren Willaims, Planet Earth Pictures, (inset)
Dr Fred Espenak, Science Photo Library p39 (left) Ian
Beames, Ardea London Ltd, (right) Mark Edwards, Still
Pictures p40 Dr Gene Feldman, NASA GSFC/Science Photo
Library p41 Hank Morgan, Science Photo Library p43 NASA/
Science Photo Library

Contents

Words printed in **bold** in the text are
explained in the glossary on page 44.

INTRODUCTION

When rubbish is dumped on the land, or oil is spilled in the sea, the land or sea is polluted. Pollution spoils a clean and healthy **environment**. The substances that pollute the environment are called pollutants. Sometimes pollutants are completely new to the environment, such as rubbish and oil. Sometimes a pollutant is a natural substance, but people use too much of it, for example, some chemicals that are found naturally in plants are added by farmers to the soil as **fertilisers**. This is when these chemicals become pollutants.

Some environments seem very unspoilt. It is hard to think that the Sahara Desert or the Antarctic are not clean. But there are no places left on Earth that are not polluted. Industry, farming, cars and even our homes all add pollutants to the Earth. The air and water carry these pollutants to all corners of the Earth.

A chain of events

Today we see many television and newspaper reports about pollution. But only 30 years ago people did not know much about pollution. In 1962, an American scientist called Rachel Carson wrote a book called *Silent Spring*. Rachel Carson wrote about the effects of a chemical called DDT. Farmers used to spray DDT on their crops to kill

Rubbish left by people pollutes the icy Antarctic.

harmful insects. But the chemical also went into the soil, and into the plants that grew on the soil. It passed into the small animals that ate the plants, and then to the birds that ate the small animals. This chain of events meant that the DDT poisoned not only the insects, but also plants and animals.

DDT was eventually banned. Today, all around the world, scientists are trying to find ways to cut down pollution. But we must all try hard to make the Earth a cleaner place.

Stone Age hunting. Even early peoples changed their environment (see page 6).

Mexico City in Central America is the most polluted city in the world.

CHAPTER ONE

SPOILING THE EARTH

Stone Age people

The earliest people on Earth lived by hunting animals and collecting nuts and berries for food. They used simple tools made of stone. This is why this period is often called the Stone Age. There were not many people in the world, so the effect on the Earth's environment was not great.

But even these few people produced some changes. They lit fires and burned down forests, and they hunted animals. So although the earliest people did not cause pollution, they did begin to change the balance between plants and animals and their environments.

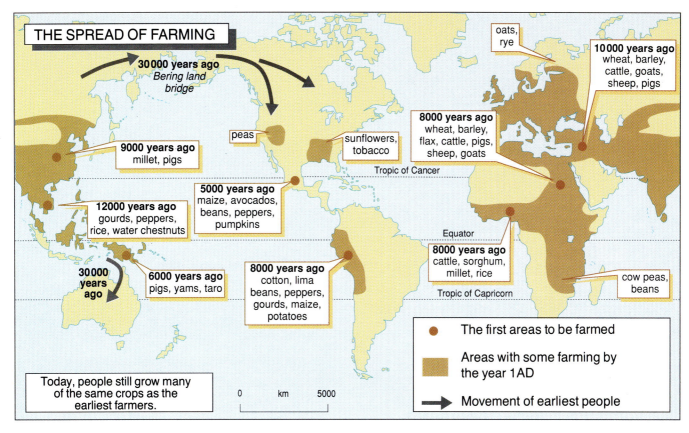

THE SPREAD OF FARMING

30 000 years ago
Bering land bridge

oats, rye

10 000 years ago
wheat, barley, cattle, goats, sheep, pigs

peas

9000 years ago
millet, pigs

sunflowers, tobacco

8000 years ago
wheat, barley, flax, cattle, pigs, sheep, goats

Tropic of Cancer

5000 years ago
maize, avocados, beans, peppers, pumpkins

12000 years ago
gourds, peppers, rice, water chestnuts

Equator

8000 years ago
cattle, sorghum, millet, rice

30 000 years ago

6000 years ago
pigs, yams, taro

8000 years ago
cotton, lima beans, peppers, gourds, maize, potatoes

Tropic of Capricorn

cow peas, beans

• The first areas to be farmed

Areas with some farming by the year 1AD

→ Movement of earliest people

Today, people still grow many of the same crops as the earliest farmers.

0   km   5000

Pollution and disease

About 10,000 years ago, people began to learn how to farm crops. Instead of moving around from place to place to look for food, people settled in villages. Later, these villages grew to become larger towns. In towns, waste such as sewage began to pollute the environment. This led to the spread of diseases. Rats, fleas and other pests made their homes in towns. This was the beginning of the age of pollution. However, worldwide the total amount of pollution was still quite small.

About 10,000 years ago people began to grow crops and settle in villages.

Pollution from mines

The next step in the story of pollution was when people discovered how to heat certain kinds of rock to **extract** metals. This is called smelting. It happened about 5000 years ago. People dug the rocks out of the ground. This is called mining.

People used metals to make tools and weapons. The waste from mining and smelting was dumped on to the land. This waste was often poisonous. The poisons from the waste ran into rivers, lakes and streams, killing animals and birds.

Other kinds of pollution also began. In Britain, by the 1200s, people used coal in their houses for heat and cooking. The coal smoke polluted the air in towns and cities. The pollution was so bad that in the time of King Edward I (1272-1307) and Queen Elizabeth I (1558-1603) there were laws to stop people burning coal in London. But coal was cheap, so no one took much notice.

New power, new pollution

In the 17th century, an Englishman called John Evelyn wrote two books about

John Evelyn wrote two books about the dangers of pollution.

pollution. The first book was about reducing smoke pollution in London. The second book was a plan to save woodlands. But before anyone could test Evelyn's ideas, a change took place that was to bring more pollution.

This change is known as the Industrial Revolution. It started in Britain in the late 1700s. Coal was burned to provide steam power. Steam power was used to drive machines and engines in factories. The Industrial Revolution soon spread to other parts of Europe and to the USA.

The Industrial Revolution was also a pollution

revolution. The waste from industries poured on to the land, into the air and into rivers and seas. Most people forgot John Evelyn's warnings.

Town plans

By the late 1900s, the large cities of the industrial countries were dirty, polluted places. Many poor people lived in cramped, badly built houses. Children often died young and many people suffered from disease. At this time, some people began to look for ways to improve city life.

In the 1820s, smoke polluted the air around coal mines.
Frenchman Le Corbusier drew this 1920s plan for a clean city with open spaces.

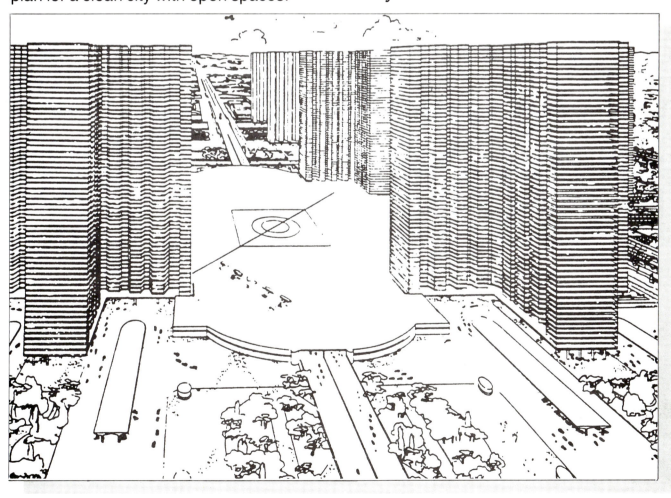

In Britain, Ebenezer Howard said that people should live in 'garden cities' – new cities built in the countryside. In France, Tony Garnier said that industry should be moved away from the cities to special areas. In Italy, a group of **architects** said that old cities should be knocked down and new cities built with wide streets, tower blocks and open spaces. In Europe and the USA people have tried out these ideas.

These changes have improved people's lives. But they have not helped to cut down pollution. Instead, people now make many new kinds of pollution. These include the exhaust fumes from cars and lorries, and chemicals used on farms to kill weeds and insects. The **developed countries** of the world cause most of the pollution. The **developing countries** produce very little pollution – so far!

A coal mine in Germany (below). After the coal has been taken out, a machine (right) puts back the earth. Then the land is planted with crops. The first crop is lucerne (see page 11).

Giving nature a hand

Over many years, plants can change so that they can grow in a polluted environment. But this is a very slow process. People produce new kinds of pollution so quickly that nature often cannot change quickly enough. Now, scientists have found ways to alter plants so that they can grow in polluted areas. This is one way that people can give nature a hand.

All over the Earth, pollution is damaging the natural world. People are trying to find ways to reduce pollution and protect nature. This is called **conservation**.

Lucerne is often planted on polluted land. It has long roots which bring plant food to the surface. This helps other plants to grow. Scientists can change plants (inset) so that they can grow on polluted land more easily.

CHAPTER TWO

TURNING POINTS

Some events during the last few years have made people think hard about what is happening to the Earth's environment. These events are often accidents, such as oil tankers spilling oil in the sea. Many of these events have changed the way we do things (see page 14). They are turning points on the path to repairing the damage done by pollution.

One of the worst accidents happened in India in 1984 at a chemical factory in a place called Bhopal. The accident killed 3300 people. It injured between 100,000 and 250,000 people.

At about the same time, some people found out that chemical waste from developed countries was being dumped in developing countries in Africa. The people in Africa did not know what was inside the barrels of waste. So they were emptying the chemicals out and using the barrels to collect water. This made them very ill.

The events in India and Africa have made governments more strict about safety and getting rid of waste in industry.

A new turn

Smog is a mixture of smoke, fog and chemical fumes. Smogs were once common in London. The worst smog was in December 1952. It was so bad that it became a turning point. More than 2000 people died. As a result, the government passed a law called the Clean Air Act. It limited coal fires and rubbish fires. Gradually, London air became cleaner.

Pittsburgh in the USA. Pittsburgh was one of the first industrial towns in Europe and the USA to bring pollution under control.

The Great London Smog

Someone who was there remembers the worst smog in London:

'In 1952 I was a student in London. The morning of December 5 had been fine and clear, sunny but cold. About two o'clock in the afternoon I was looking out of the window over the Thames when I noticed a strong, dark line had appeared across the sky. Gradually, over the next hour it began to get dark. What looked like smoke began to curl into the room through an open window. It smelled strongly of coal smoke.

The next day the fog became even thicker. Street lights were no help at all. Gradually traffic disappeared. London became a silent, dead city. Then the fog began to change. The grey, thick mist turned yellow and began to smell, or rather taste, very bad. Breathing in was likely to give you a sharp pain in the lungs and if you were suffering from a cold then you could expect a terrible cough, with no fresh air anywhere.

When the fog finally began to lift, on the following Tuesday, we saw a really strange sight. The common opposite our house was covered with cars, lorries and buses. One or two had even gone into the duck ponds.'

December 1952: a London bus is led through the fog by a conductor carrying a flare.

On the road to a cleaner future?

These are some of the most important turning points of the past 50 years on the road to a cleaner world.

Toxin explosion in West Virginia, USA. New laws to make chemical industries safer.
1949

1947
Smoke control laws introduced in Pittsburg, USA.

Great London Smog. Clean-up of smoke begins.
1952

NUCLEAR BOMB TESTS
(by USA, USSR, Britain and France)

Clean Air Act passed in Britain.
1958

1952
The first victory for a conservation group in Britain: English fishing clubs gain the right to have clean rivers and lakes.

1957
Poor design of nuclear power station leads to nuclear accident in England.

1959
Extent of nuclear fallout from 1957 accident revealed. Nuclear power stations modified.

World community agrees to Montreal Protocol to reduce use of CFCs, in order to protect ozone layer.
1987

Nuclear accident at Chernobyl, in USSR.
1986

Explosion at chemical factory in Bhopal, India, kills thousands. Many countries take action to increase safety in factory-building in poor countries.
NASA scientists announce that greenhouse effect is real.
First North Sea Conference agrees to clean up the North Sea.
Catalytic converters fitted on American cars to reduce exhaust fumes.
1984

1988
International conference on climate reaches agreement to reduce pollution caused by greenhouse gases. Britain sets up National Rivers Authority to control quality of all water.

1985
British scientists discover that pollution is causing a hole in the ozone layer over the Antarctic.

1980-82
Effect of acid rain on rivers and lakes discovered. European Community directives on quality of drinking water.

1989
First World Climate Conference recognises greenhouse threat. Strong resolution to reduce greenhouse gas pollution.

1990
New pollution controls and new schemes to recycle waste in many industrial countries.
Britain abandons plans to build new nuclear power stations.
Second World Climate Conference reinforces measures to control greenhouse gases.

When the Cold War ended in 1989-1990, the extent of pollution in eastern Europe, including the former USSR, was finally revealed. To reach a cleaner world in the twenty-first century the industries of eastern Europe will have to invest effort and money to match the standards now being imposed in western Europe, USA, Canada and Japan.

Nuclear Test Ban treaty signed by USA, USSR and Britain. Ban stops most tests above ground.
1963

International group called Club of Rome produces influential report showing that pollution will increase if industry grows without making changes in production methods.
1969

NUCLEAR BOMB TESTS
(by China and India)

1962
Silent Spring published. Bans imposed on some agricultural chemicals in USA and Europe.

1967
Canada controls inland water pollution and Canada and USA set up commission on the Great Lakes and St Lawrence River pollution.

Three Mile Island nuclear accident forces USA to abandon nuclear power. Sweden also abandons nuclear power. Houses in USA discovered to have been built on worst toxic waste dump in the country. Strict regulations on dumping introduced.
1979

Computer-based forecast *Limits to Growth*, published in USA, confirms link between industrial growth and pollution.
1972

European Community directives on quality of water for swimming.
1976

UK Control of Pollution Act passed.
1974

1970
Environmental Protection Agency founded in the USA. Royal Commission on Environmental Pollution set up in Britain. Great public interest in pollution matters.

1973
First oil shock as price triples in one year. Many energy-saving measures introduced in USA, Europe and Japan, which reduce pollution.

1978
Second oil shock as price increases. New energy-saving measures introduced.

1975
Mediterranean Action Plan by countries bordering the sea to control pollution.

1990s
This new decade marks the beginning of the Age of Conservation. Many scientific and government organisations are now ready to tackle the main problems of pollution worldwide. However it is not a straight road to a green future. Major disasters such as the Gulf War, may create new turning points.

1992
World Environment Conference in Rio de Janeiro. World leaders met to map out new schemes for world environment conservation.

Acid rain

After the Clean Air Act in Britain (see page 12), coal was not used so much in homes. But coal was still burned in power stations. People built tall chimneys on top of these power stations to try to get rid of the coal smoke. Other countries such as Germany, Belgium and Holland also built power stations with tall chimneys. The smoke from the chimneys is full of gases. These gases dissolve in cloud droplets in the Earth's atmosphere. When the cloud droplets join together to make raindrops, acid rain forms.

Acid rain has damaged conifer trees in North Carolina, USA.
A factory in Romania fills the air with soot and gases affecting people and animals.

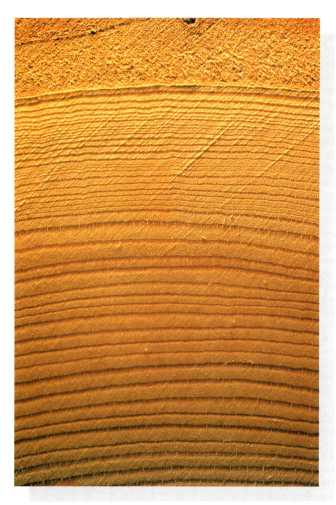

The outer rings of the this tree (at the top) are very narrow. They show that the growth of the tree has been affected, probably by acid rain.

In the 1970s, people in Scandinavia noticed that fish in the lakes and rivers were dying. Trees were also beginning to die. Scientists found out that acid rain was poisoning the fish and trees. Although the power stations were far away in Britain, Belgium, Germany and Holland, their pollution was affecting forests and lakes in Scandinavia.

In 1987 the western European countries agreed to clean up the coal smoke before it was released. This will cost a lot of money and will take a long time.

A new threat from the air

In Britain at the end of the 1980s, doctors noticed that the number of children with asthma was increasing. It seemed to get worse in the summer. Doctors in Los Angeles, California, USA noticed the same thing. They think it is caused by strong sunlight reacting with car exhaust fumes to produce new chemicals in the air. This is called photochemical smog.

When the smog is worst in Los Angeles, there are warnings to people with asthma to stay indoors. Doctors in Britain also think that the increase in asthma is caused by sunlight and exhaust fumes. There are now smog warnings in Britain.

However, by 1994 the atmosphere had got a little cleaner. Nobody is really sure why this happened, but many countries are now working to improve the atmosphere. Some are developing new kinds of power, using the sun, the waves and the wind.

CHAPTER THREE

TROUBLED WATERS

The map opposite shows the areas of the world which are in special danger from oil pollution. Sometimes oil is spilled while tankers load and unload. Oil also escapes from oil wells where oil is being mined in the sea. At other times, oil is spilled when an oil tanker is damaged in storms at sea. But most oil pollution is caused on purpose or by carelessness.

For example, a ship's captain sometimes orders the crew to clean out the tanks of an empty tanker at sea. This is not legal, but it saves time and money.

In 1989, a tanker called the *Exxon Valdez* spilt its load of oil in the clean waters of Prince William Sound, Alaska, USA. Rocks in shallow water had ripped the hull of the tanker open when

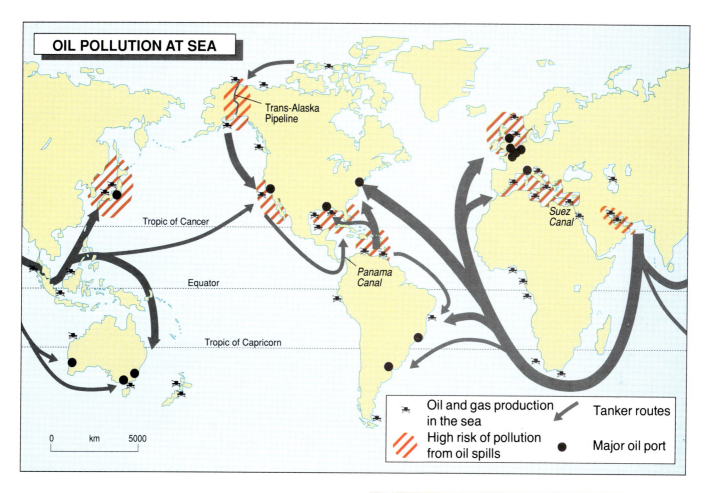

OIL POLLUTION AT SEA

Trans-Alaska Pipeline

Tropic of Cancer

Equator

Panama Canal

Suez Canal

Tropic of Capricorn

0   km   5000

	Oil and gas production in the sea		Tanker routes
	High risk of pollution from oil spills		Major oil port

it went too near to the shore. The oil ruined one of the most unspoilt areas on Earth.

In 1991, during the Gulf War, huge amounts of oil were poured into the sea. The oil made a slick five times bigger than the one caused by the *Exxon Valdez*. In 1992 in Spain and in 1993 in Scotland, tankers were wrecked and almost as much oil was spilled as from the *Exxon Valdez*.

At sea, a plastic inflatable barrier is used to trap spilled oil (left).
Spilt oil kills sea birds (centre right).
Cleaning oil from a beach (right).

River check

The River Tees in northeast England is 180 kilometres long. It is like many rivers in industrial countries. Clean water at the top of the river is stored in reservoirs. Waste water is put back into the river further down. This pollutes the lower parts of the river. Factories beside the river can also cause pollution.

When this reservoir was built it destroyed the most important area of rare alpine plants in Britain. The blue gentian (see below) was one of the flowers affected.

In 1984, chemicals from this quarry leaked into the river. The chemicals killed all the fish and animals for 50 kilometres downstream.

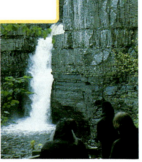

High Force Waterfall attracts many visitors. Their rubbish pollutes the water.

Peat on the moors colours the water, not pollution. The water used to be too polluted for salmon to live in the river, but the river is now clean enough for salmon once again.

Farm waste pollutes the river in the summer.

Barnard Castle

Blue gentian (see above)

Polluted water

Clean water

A river in Italy
The River Po is fed partly by clean water from the mountains around it. Water is taken from the river for industry and for drinking. The river is polluted by industrial and farming waste and sewage. In some places, special treatments are needed to clean the water in the river.

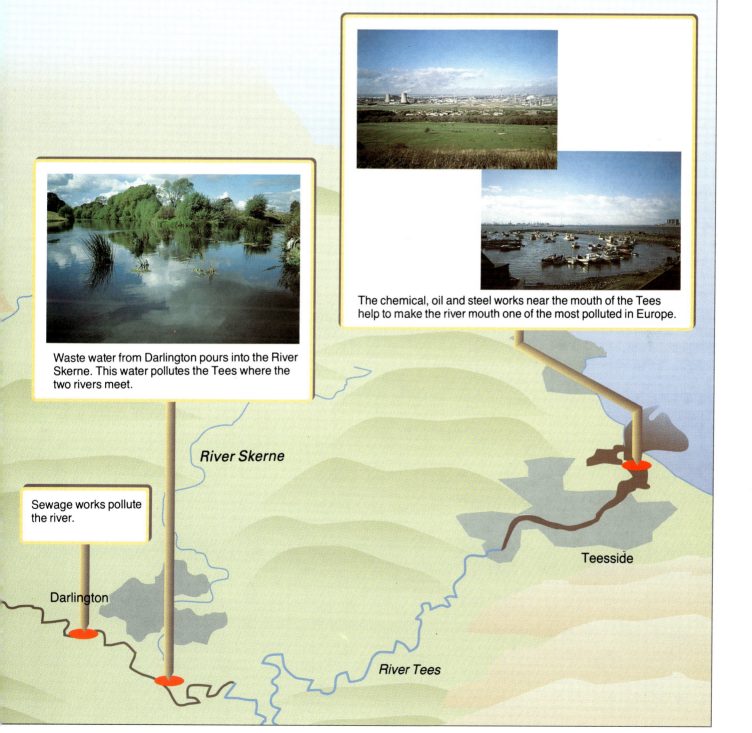

The chemical, oil and steel works near the mouth of the Tees help to make the river mouth one of the most polluted in Europe.

Waste water from Darlington pours into the River Skerne. This water pollutes the Tees where the two rivers meet.

Sewage works pollute the river.

River Skerne

Darlington

Teesside

River Tees

CHAPTER FOUR

NUCLEAR DISASTER

At 1.30 in the morning on Friday 25 April 1986 an accident happened at the Chernobyl nuclear power station in the Ukraine (in what was then the USSR). It was the world's most dangerous accident ever.

At the heart of a nuclear power station is a nuclear reactor. Inside the reactor a special kind of fuel slowly breaks down, giving off huge amounts of energy as it does so. In a nuclear power station, the energy is used to heat water to make steam. The steam drives machines called generators that make electricity.

Dangerous experiment
The day of the accident at Chernobyl, an operator turned off the emergency water cooling system to the reactor to do an experiment on one of the generators. Nobody switched the cooling system back on again! This was the first of six mistakes.

At 1.22am, a computer printed out a mass of figures. The figures showed that the reactor was in danger of overheating. If nothing was done there would be a huge surge of steam. Nobody noticed the warning.

By this time, operators had also removed many of the rods that cool the reactor. Only at the last moment did the operators realise the danger. In panic, they dropped the rods back into the reactor – but it was too late. The 1661 rods of uranium fuel were red-hot. They broke from their metal containers and mixed with the steam. Huge explosions followed, breaking the floor, walls and roof of the reactor building. A fire broke out sending clouds of deadly smoke into the air.

The control room in the Chernobyl nuclear power station (top). This is where the first warnings of danger were given.
The Chernobyl nuclear power station (centre). The explosion happened in the reactor beside the tall chimney. Helicopters were used to put out the fire (bottom).

First reactions

Police and fire services rushed to the burning building. A policeman described it later:

'Near the bridge the car drove into either fog or dust – nothing could be seen over two metres and we drove blind. Near the main office building "speedies" (ambulancemen) almost at a run were carrying someone on a stretcher. We found the doctor of the plant but he shrugged his shoulders.'

The local people asleep in their beds knew nothing of the fire. The power station was some kilometres away. But dust from the reactor fire fell on to the villages and towns around Chernobyl. This dust was very dangerous because it was **radioactive**. Radioactive dust can kill people if they breathe it in. The following Monday, schools asked mothers to collect their children early. They had been told to get ready to leave Chernobyl. The Russian authorities had not told the local people the truth about the Chernobyl fire. One woman learned about the accident from a neighbour.

After the accident at Chernobyl, people hosed down the buildings in villages nearby to try to remove the dangerous radioactive chemicals.

The amount of radioactivity in fields near Chernobyl is checked by special machines called geiger counters.

A deadly cloud

The explosion at Chernobyl produced a huge cloud of deadly radioactive dust. This cloud soon spread as the wind blew it across Europe. In power stations in Sweden there are machines to tell operators how much radioactivity there is in the air. Late Saturday and early Sunday after the explosion these machines began to sound the alarm. The Swedes realised that the radioactivity was coming from outside the power stations.

In Britain, the dust fell in heavy rain on the hills in parts of Wales, the Lake District and Scotland. The radioactive chemicals went into the hill plants and passed on to the sheep who ate these plants. These sheep had to be killed. In 1994 some sheep were still being harmed by radioactive chemicals in the soil and could not be sold.

In northern Sweden there was a similar story. The radioactive chemicals went into plants called lichens. The lichens are food for herds of reindeer. Even six years after the accident, there was still too much radioactivity and the reindeer were all killed.

After the accident

Many people have already died as a result of the Chernobyl accident. The operators who were so careless were very close to the explosion. Many of them died from poisoning from the radioactive chemicals. The brave firemen and helicopter pilots who fought the fire have also suffered. Many of them are sick and dying. They are true heroes because they stopped the fire from becoming worse and spreading to the other reactors in the power station.

Nobody knows how many people will die because of the explosion. But the people who are affected most by the radioactive chemicals are the local children. So many are ill that there is not enough space left in Ukrainian hospitals for them. As one Russian man said:

'At first the Soviet government did not tell us what was happening and we could not find out the extent of it because we had no equipment to monitor it. Now we can see it in ourselves. The children do not laugh or run and play. They sit around in groups like old men.'

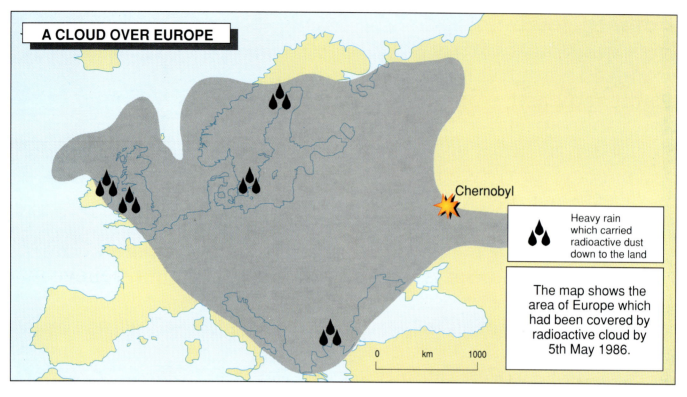

A CLOUD OVER EUROPE

Chernobyl

Heavy rain which carried radioactive dust down to the land

The map shows the area of Europe which had been covered by radioactive cloud by 5th May 1986.

0   km   1000

Turning against nuclear power

Chernobyl was not the first nuclear accident. There was an accident in Britain in 1957, and one in the USA in 1979.

The American accident happened at a power station at Three Mile Island in Pennsylvania. On 28 March 1979 the water that cools the reactor shut off. The operators tried to open it again, but they failed. Luckily, there was no explosion and no radioactive chemicals escaped from the power station. But unlike at Chernobyl, the authorities told the people around the power station about the accident. The reaction of the local people astonished the authorities. About 144,000 people ran away from the area. As one man said:

'They said we'd be OK but what the heck do they know? I just got my family in the car and went like a bat out of hell.'

It took six years to make the power station at Three Mile Island completely safe. Since the accident no new nuclear power stations have been built in the USA.

Other countries have also said that they will not use nuclear power. They include Australia, Iceland, Norway, Luxemburg, Portugal, New Zealand and Ireland.

In favour of nuclear power

Some countries still believe in nuclear power. They include France, Belgium, Germany and Japan. Japan plans to build another 30 to 40 power stations. These countries argue that if stations are properly run they are safe. They also say that people are more likely to become ill from pollution in the air than from radioactive chemicals from nuclear power stations.

Which countries are right about nuclear power? Is it safe or not? We cannot answer these questions yet. But we do know that all these countries have the problem of what to do with nuclear waste from the reactors. But the worst nuclear pollution comes from nuclear bomb-making and testing. In 1994 in the USA, for example, 1377 sites were polluted by nuclear waste from bomb-making.

The Saami (Lapp) people live in northern Scandinavia. They were forced to kill their herds of reindeer after the accident at Chernobyl.

A history lesson

At present, most nuclear waste is stored under the ground. The waste is put into shallow pits or holes full of water. The waste is radioactive, so it must not touch any water or air. If it did there would be a huge explosion. Some radioactive waste will last a long time, so it will be dangerous for thousands of years to come.

One idea to get rid of dangerous waste is to turn it into a kind of glass. The glass holds the dangerous radioactive chemicals apart from each other. But this idea is still at the early stages. The most common way to get rid of waste is to bury it deep under the ground. The waste is put into metal containers. No water must get inside the containers, so the metal must be very strong. It must be able to last for thousands of years. Do scientists know whether metal can last this long without rotting?

Some radioactive waste is buried in shallow pits.

Scientists are doing experiments to turn radioactive waste into glass.

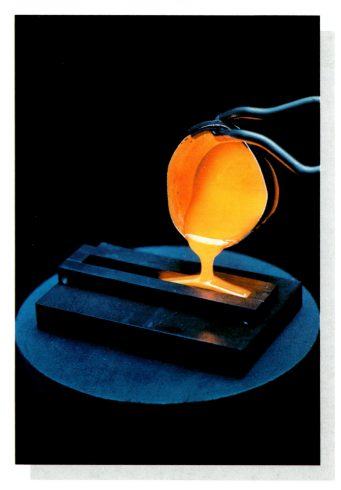

Scientists are studying ancient armour made from bronze to find out how metal ages.

This cave near Washington, USA could be used to store nuclear waste. The cave is made from a very hard rock called basalt.

To find out, scientists are studying ancient metal. They have found some iron nails buried by the ancient Romans nearly 2000 years ago. The nails have hardly rotted at all. Scientists are also studying even older metal used by the ancient Greeks for making armour.

The arguments for and against nuclear power will go on for many years to come. But people have learned a hard lesson from the accident at Chernobyl.

CHAPTER FIVE

MORE PEOPLE, MORE POLLUTION

Every year, the number of people in the world grows. Now there are about 5000 million people. By 2020, there will be about 7000 million. Scientists are trying to work out how to grow enough food for all these people. Some scientists think farmers must put more chemicals on their fields to make more crops grow. Others say these extra chemicals will increase pollution. But now there are new ways to increase food supplies without pollution.

The photograph on the opposite page shows a new kind of 'farm'. It produces chemicals that people and animals can eat. One of these chemicals is a white powder that is a form of protein. The cows in the picture eat the powder and it keeps them healthy. People can eat this food, too. Scientists add flavours and vitamins so that it tastes good and provides everything humans need.

The white food powder is made from a liquid called methanol. And methanol is made from waste products of the oil industry. **Fungi** and **bacteria** turn methanol into the powder when they eat it. But ordinary fungi and bacteria cannot do this. First, scientists have to change

Scientists have used genetic engineering to alter the seeds in this seed bank.

This factory makes an artificial food which the cows eat.

them using a technique called **genetic engineering**.

Genetic engineering is used to change the genes of plants and animals. Genes are chemical 'instructions'. They exist in the cells of all living things and tell them what to do. If scientists change the genes of the fungi and bacteria, they can produce the special food powder. In the future, scientists will probably use genetic engineering to make many different foods.

Nitrates mean more food

Plants need water and minerals to grow. Minerals are special chemicals in the soil. The most important mineral for plants is nitrogen.

Nitrogen is a gas in the air. But it is also in soil, where it is joined to other chemicals. These combinations are called nitrates. Scientists discovered that if they put more nitrates on the soil, more crops grew. So in the 1920s, they started to make nitrate fertilisers in factories.

Over the last 20 years, farmers have put too many nitrates on their fields. The crops cannot use them all. Rain has washed some of the extra nitrates into rivers. The rest have sunk into water under the ground. Now in Europe and the USA, they are causing serious pollution.

Small lumps on these broad bean roots contain bacteria. These bacteria make nitrates in the soil.

The reeds in marshes next to rivers soak up fertilisers.

Nitrates: a threat to health

Nitrates are dangerous for two reasons. They cause cancer in people and they make water plants such as algae grow too fast. These plants quickly use up all the oxygen in the rivers so that fish die. When blue-green algae mix with nitrates, they become dangerous. They can poison fish in the rivers. Some people in Finland and the former USSR died when they ate these poisoned fish.

Marshes at the edge of rivers can soak up nitrates. In the 1980s, people drained the marshes around the river Skjer in Denmark to create more farmland. As a result, more nitrates flowed into the river. Algae quickly grew and used up all the oxygen in the water. Many fish died. Now the Danish government is putting the marshes back.

Biological control

Biological control means using nature to fight pollution. In Australia, scientists are using it to fight screw worm flies. These flies lay their eggs in the skin of cows. When they hatch, the grubs eat the cows' flesh and make sores on their skin. Then other diseases infect the sores. Now scientists are breeding millions of infertile male flies. (Infertile flies cannot produce young.) These flies mate with females, but the eggs the females lay will not grow. The screw worm flies may soon die out.

Farmers use biological control in Thailand, too. They breed fish to live in flooded rice fields. These fish eat the grubs of insects so that they cannot destroy the rice plants. This is much cheaper than using insecticides to control pests. The farmers can sell the fish to make money, too.

Farmers breed fish to eat insects in their paddy fields where rice is grown.

In the future, farmers will use more biological control methods and fewer harmful pesticides. Scientists are using genetic engineering to produce wheat, soya beans and other crops that can make their own fertiliser. If they are successful, farmers will use less nitrate fertiliser.

Safe to eat?

Farmers spray fruit and vegetables with chemicals to stop insects and other pests damaging them. By the time we eat the food, only a small amount of chemicals remains. Scientists have tested all the chemicals to make sure small amounts are safe for people to eat. But the chemicals may build up in our bodies over a long period of time. Nobody knows if this is dangerous.

Politicians, scientists and farmers are now working to cut down the amount of chemicals used in farming. The USA bans many chemicals that cause cancer in animals. In Sweden, farmers have halved the amount of pesticides they use.

Using fewer chemicals does not mean that farms produce fewer crops. In Sweden, organic farming methods are very successful. (Organic farmers use only natural manures and no chemical sprays.) They produce the same amount of crops as the old methods. The farmers make more money, too, by spending less on chemicals.

These new farming methods will probably become much more common in the rich countries of the world. One study says that by 2020, half our food will contain no artificial chemicals.

Farmers spray most fruit (left) with chemicals.

Mixed farming (right) uses animal manures to help fertilise the soil. This is much less polluting than using only chemicals.

CHAPTER SIX

DESIGNS FOR THE FUTURE

In the past, many industries were dirty and dangerous. People put up with the pollution because the industries provided jobs and money. But now people want to live in a clean, safe world where industries are successful without polluting the environment.

Many countries in western Europe and the USA now have strong laws against pollution. Engineers are also improving the design of factories and products to make them cleaner and safer.

Cars are one of the main causes of pollution. Now engineers are making cleaner engines that use less fuel. In Germany and Holland there are new, low speed limits in cities, too. Cars have to travel

This car, Sunraycer, uses solar power (power from the Sun).

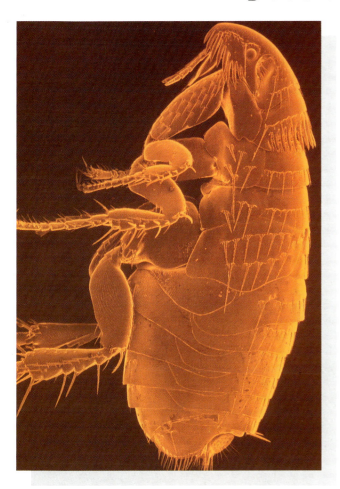

Fleas can jump many times higher than their own bodies. Scientists are studying how these insects release so much energy.

all industries will be cleaner so that the world becomes a safer place.

Ideas from coral

Some animals and plants use energy and food very efficiently. Now scientists are studying their secrets to see if they can help industry to be more efficient, too.

Many tiny coral animals live in the oceans. But the water often contains very little of the chemicals they need to grow. These chemicals are called phosphates.

In the 1980s, engineers studied the coral of Great Barrier Reef in Australia. They discovered that the corals were taking phosphates from the water ten times more efficiently than a factory could. The corals did this partly by a chemical process. But it was their special surface that made the process so efficient. This type of surface is called a 'fractal' surface (see photograph on the next page). A fractal surface is folded over on itself many times, like a concertina. If you flattened the surface out, it would cover a huge area. The corals are able to use all this area to take in phosphates.

at the same speed as bicycles. These limits will cut down pollution. Designers are also producing new cars for slow city driving. The new cars are powered by an electric motor and a diesel engine. Drivers use the electric motor in cities and the diesel engine outside. Electric cars do not produce fumes that pollute city streets.

If all these new ideas are successful, the car industry will soon cause much less pollution. By the twenty-first century, scientists hope that

Scientists believe that fractal surfaces could make many chemical processes more efficient. In a car battery, for example, metal sheets react with acid to make an electric current. If the sheets had fractal surfaces, the battery would produce more electricity and last longer.

Small is beautiful
Making materials to build machines can cause pollution. Industrial designers are trying to produce smaller, more efficient machines to reduce this problem. For example,

The patterns of corals (below) and fractals (computer image, inset) may help engineers to design efficient machines.

This river (right) is polluted with mercury, a metal. Acorn powder contains a chemical that attracts heavy metals. In the future acorns (above) may be used to clean polluted water.

the invention of tiny electronic microchips made it possible to produce small computers. And we can now send phone messages down thin glass wires instead of heavy metal cables, using a technique called fibreoptics.

New discoveries about chemicals help designers to produce more efficient machines. A new chemical called gallium arsenide can make electricity from sunlight. In 1990 scientists put it into the plastic coating of a small aircraft. This aircraft flew right across the USA in 40 days. The gallium arsenide produced all the electricity it needed. Scientists have also discovered that if they add iodine to plastic, it can transmit electricity. Soon they hope to replace harmful metal electricity cables with plastic.

Smaller, lighter machines need less energy to make them work. About 30 years ago, industrial countries began to forecast how much energy they would need in the future. All the forecasts were too high. This is because new designs and materials have made machines smaller and more efficient. So they use less energy.

CHAPTER SEVEN

WORLD PROBLEMS WORLD SOLUTIONS

About 100 years ago, some scientists began to warn people about what we now call the 'greenhouse effect'. They said that cars and industries were producing too many waste gases such as carbon dioxide. These gases were letting in the Sun's heat. But like the glass in a greenhouse, they were not letting it out again. The scientists believed the greenhouse effect would make the Earth hotter. Ice in the North and South Poles would melt. Then the seas would rise and flood the land. Many scientists think this process is now beginning.

Pollution can be watched from space. This **false-colour satellite picture** shows where plants are growing. On the land, the green areas have most plants. In the sea, the red areas have the most, pink the least.

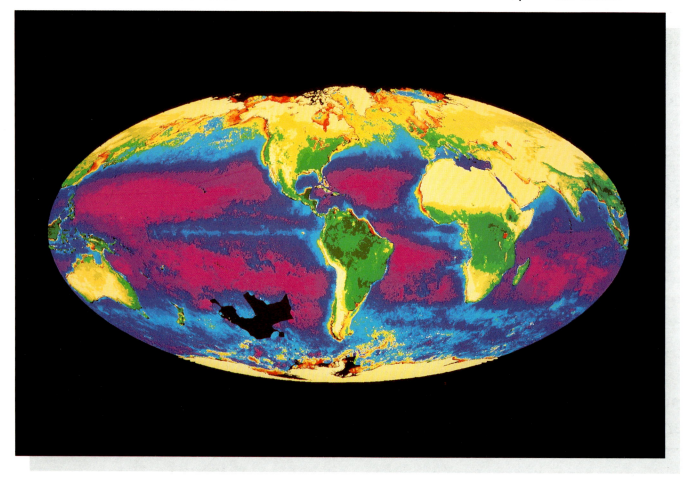

Methane gas from a rubbish dump fuels this power station in California, USA.

The greenhouse threat

Burning coal, oil and gas to produce electricity is a main cause of the greenhouse effect. Now scientists are looking for new energy sources. In California, USA, wind is already used to power 15,000 electricity generators. Solar power is also becoming more popular.

The wind and the Sun are called renewable energy sources because they do not run out like fossil fuels. In 1994, the British government promised to develop wind power and other renewable energy sources such as rubbish burning and gas from waste heaps. New Zealand, the USA and other countries tap the heat stored in rocks inside the Earth. This is known as hot rock power.

Hydro-electric power uses the renewable power of moving water to generate electricity. By 2020, it will produce about one fifth of the world's energy.

Turning down the fires

In the future, waste materials may drive power stations. Old car tyres already fuel five power stations in the USA. Engineers are also designing new gas power stations.

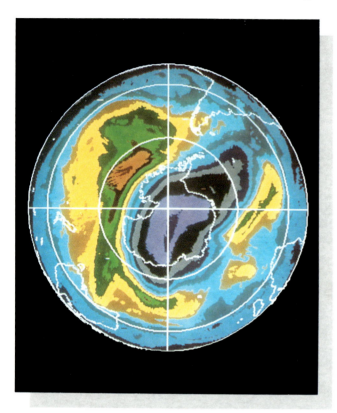

This satellite map shows the ozone layer 'hole' in dark blue, purple, black and grey.

Pollution protocol
In 1987, the polluting countries of the world signed a document called the Montreal Protocol. In it, they agreed to cut down the production of gases called chlorofluorocarbons (CFCs for short).

Until recently, CFCs were used to cool refrigerators and to push sprays out of aerosol cans. Scientists now know they are dangerous because they destroy the ozone layer around the Earth. Ozone is a special form of oxygen that exists high up in the atmosphere. It absorbs ultra-violet rays from the Sun, which are harmful to people, animals and plants. Because the ozone layer now has a 'hole' in it, more rays are reaching the Earth. The Montreal Protocol means we now produce fewer CFCs. But the CFCs already in the air will cause damage for a long time to come.

This book shows that the problem of pollution can be overcome. There are ways to clean up the Earth and to keep it clean in the future. We all depend on our planet, so we must all care for it.

In them, the gas drives the electricity generators. Then it is reused to heat the power stations themselves. Methane gas from old underground rubbish dumps may also be used to make power.

Planting trees can reduce the greenhouse effect because trees take in carbon dioxide from the air.

Recycling waste materials will also reduce pollution. People already reuse paper, aluminium, glass and plastic.

In all these ways, we are beginning to repair the damage caused by pollution. Now we must start to plan for the future.

Dinosaurs: victims of pollution?

Dinosaurs lived on Earth for over 100 million years. Then, 65 million years ago, they suddenly died out. Until recently, nobody knew why.

By studying rocks, scientists discovered that a layer of a chemical called iridium appeared in many different rocks all around the world. Some scientists believed that this chemical came from a meteorite. They thought this meteorite hit the Earth in the time of the dinosaurs and made them extinct.

The meteorite was probably as big as a large mountain. An object like this would hit the Earth with a great force and kill all living creatures over a land area as large as Asia. It would also make vast clouds of dust and gas. These clouds would block out the Sun for many years, making the Earth dark and cold. If this really did happen, the pollution in the air and the freezing temperatures probably killed the dinosaurs.

GLOSSARY

architect – a person who designs buildings.

bacteria – a group of single-celled plants growing in all environments. Some can cause disease, but most are important for the ecology of the Earth.

conservation – the protection of the environment and living things.

DDT – dichlorodiphenyltrichloroethane, a chemical used as an insecticide.

developed countries – a rich country with many industries.

developing countries – a poor country with little industry.

environment – the places in which plants and animals live and which provide them with everything they need.

extract – to take out.

false-colour satellite picture – a satellite picture coloured in by a computer. It does not show the real colours of objects on Earth, but highlights them with brighter, stronger shades.

fertilisers – substances added to soil to make plants grow more strongly.

fungi – a group of plants without green colour that eat dead or living plants or animals.

genetic engineering – the process of changing the genes – chemical 'instructions' – in the cells of living things.

radioactive – describes a substance that gives out radiation. Large amounts of radiation can be harmful to living things.

INDEX